P·I·C·T·U·R·E·P·E·D·I·A

NOTE TO PARENTS

This book is part of PICTUREPEDIA, a completely
new kind of information series for children.
Its unique combination of pictures and words
encourages children to use their eyes to discover and
explore the world, while introducing them to a wealth
of basic knowledge. Clear, straightforward text
explains each picture thoroughly and provides
additional information about the topic.

"Looking it up" becomes an easy task with
PICTUREPEDIA, an ideal first reference for all types of
schoolwork. Because PICTUREPEDIA is also entertaining,
children will enjoy reading its words and looking
at its pictures over and over again. You can encourage and
stimulate further inquiry by helping your child
pose simple questions for the whole family to
"look up" and answer together.

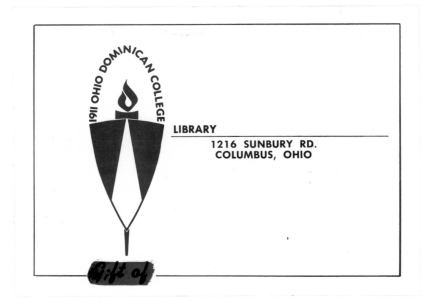

SPORTS

A DK PUBLISHING BOOK

Consultant Stan Greenberg

Senior Editor Sue Leonard
Art Editor Amanda Carroll

Series Editor Sarah Phillips
Series Art Editor Ruth Shane

Picture Researcher Miriam Sharland

Production Manager Ian Paton

Editorial Director Jonathan Reed
Design Director Ed Day

First American Edition, 1994
4 6 8 1 9 7 5 3

Published in the United States by
DK Publishing, Inc., 95 Madison Avenue
New York, New York 10016

CIP data is available.
ISBN 1-56458-640-5

Reproduced by Colourscan, Singapore
Printed and bound in Italy by Graphicom

SPORTS

CONTENTS

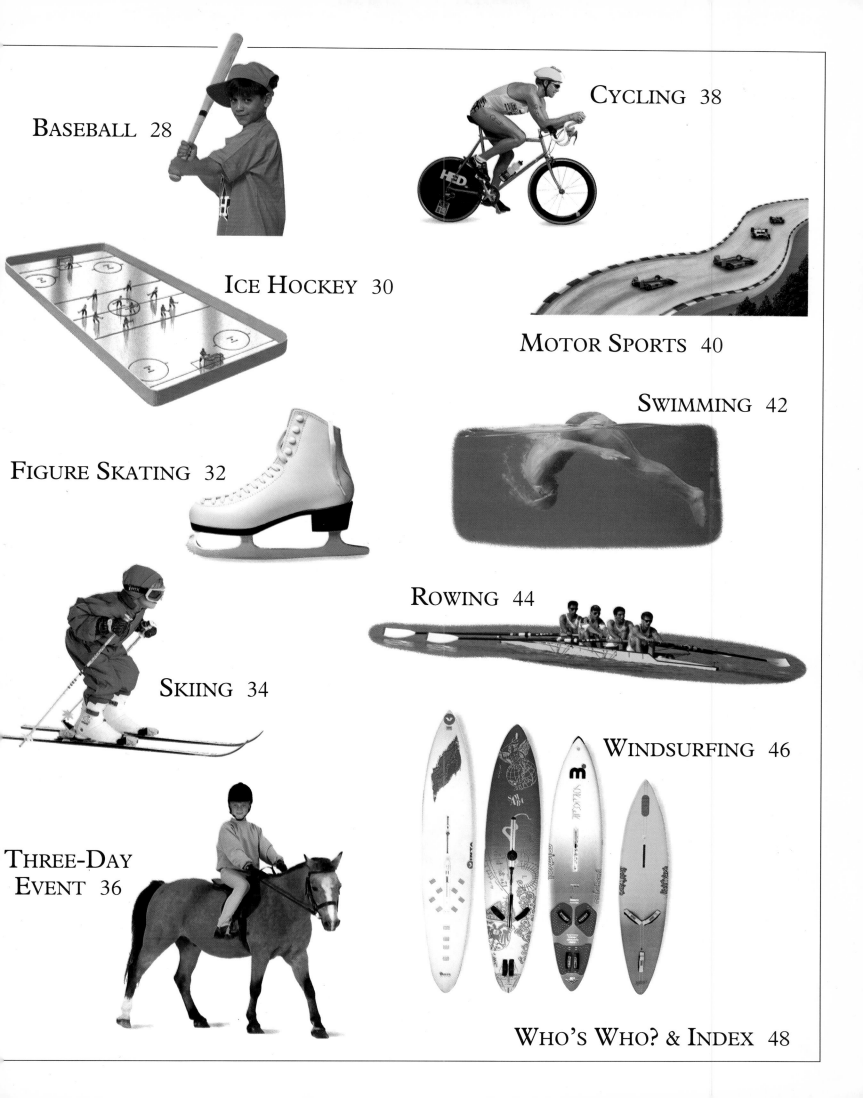

THE WORLD OF SPORTS

Every four years, the world's greatest athletes compete in the Olympics. At every Olympic Games, competitors run faster, jump higher, and create more amazing records. The Olympic ideals of honesty, sportsmanship, and pride flourish alongside these inspiring performances and spill over into the world of sports at every level.

Source of Light
The Olympic flame is carried by torch by a series of runners from Olympia in Greece to the Games arena.

Wreath

Kenyan runner William Tanui

Medal

The Ultimate Prize
At the original Olympics in ancient Greece, winners received an olive wreath. Modern Olympic champions receive a gold medal.

New Zealand show-jumper Mark Todd

Old Events
Some sports were once played at the Games but are no longer included. For example, cricket was only played at the 1900 Games in Paris, France. Shown here is a modern cricketer in Britain.

New Addition
New sports can be added to the Games. Windsurfing was only 20 years old when it became an Olympic event in 1984 – making it the youngest sport ever to be included.

Chinese diver Mingxia Fu

The Paralympic Games
Sport should be for everyone regardless of disabilities. The first full Paralympic Games were staged in Rome, Italy, in 1960. When possible, these games are held in the same country as the Olympics.

German tennis player Steffi Graf

American athlete Carl Lewis

The Colors of the World
The Olympic rings represent the five competing continents of the world. The flags of every Olympic nation contain at least one of the colors featured on the rings.

The Winter Olympics
The first modern Olympics were held in Athens, Greece, in 1896. It was not until 1924 that the winter Olympics began in Chamonix, France. They are now held two years after the summer Olympic Games.

RUNNING

As long as you are fit, you can compete in running and chasing games – but world-class athletes have to train every day as they try to run faster than anyone has ever run before. Different running events require different physical abilities. Runners in 100-yard dashes produce amazing bursts of speed over short distances. Marathon runners have to keep a relatively constant speed during races that last for hours on end.

Royal View
The 1908 Olympics were held in London, England. The marathon was run over 42,195 meters (46,415 yd.) so that it could start under the royal children's nursery at Windsor Castle. This became the standard distance.

Record Run
On May 6, 1954, Roger Bannister was the first man to run a mile (1.609 km) in under four minutes.

Start for the 200 m (220 yd.), 3,000 m (3,300 yd.) and 5,000 m (5,500 yd.)

Long-distance runners often break away from the other runners in the hope that they will not be able to catch up.

The starter calls "on your marks" and "set." Then he or she fires the starting pistol, and the athletes burst into action.

110-meter (120-yd.) hurdles start

100-m (110-yd.) and 100-m (110-yd.) hurdles start

For shorter distances, athletes use starting blocks, which help them to push off.

Relay events are usually run over four legs of 100 meters (110 yd.) or four legs of 400 meters (440 yd.). Three team members have to pass a baton to the next runner at the end of his or her leg of the race. The fourth runner crosses the finish line.

Making a Splash

Steeplechase runners jump four wooden barriers and a water jump on each of the race's seven full laps. Unlike hurdles, these barriers cannot be knocked over.

Barcelona '92

On the Right Track

A standard athletics track is 400 meters (440 yd.) around, and all races are run anticlockwise. Modern tracks are made of synthetic materials and are not affected by the weather.

Runners have spikes on the soles of their shoes that help them grip the track.

1,500-meter (1,650-yd.) start

Competitors have to jump ten hurdles for each race. In each event, the hurdles are a different height. The hurdles in the 400 meters (440 yd.) are the lowest.

Start of relays, 400-m (440-yd.) hurdles, 400 m (440 yd.), 800 m (880 yd.), and 10,000 m (11,000 yd.), and the finish for all races

100-meter (110-yd.) runners are the fastest men and women on earth. Top sprinters reach speeds of over 25 miles (40 km) an hour.

9

DECATHLON

The decathlon contest is made up of ten track and field events. Contestants have to be very fit and skilled in order to take part in so many different running, jumping, and throwing competitions. Many of the events date back to the original Olympics held at Olympia in Greece some 3,000 years ago. Modern decathletes battle against each other in order to find out who is the best all-round athlete in the world.

Testing Time
The ten decathlon events are held over two days.

100 meters
(110 yd.)

Long jump

Shot put

High jump

400 meters
(440 yd.)

110-meter
(120-yd.) hurdles

Discus

Pole vault

Javelin

1,500 meters
(1,650 yd.)

Training for War
Javelin and discus throwing were both part of the ancient Olympic Games. At that time, sports were a way of training for battle. The javelin was a weapon, and the discus was developed from a shield.

A javelin weighs 1.8 pounds (800 g) and is between 8.5 and 8.9 feet (260 and 270 cm) long.

A discus weighs 4.4 pounds (2 kg).

Heavy Weight
Male athletes use a shot weighing 16 pounds (about 7 kg) – the same as this basket of potatoes. The shot, javelin, and discus used by women are lighter than those used by the men.

A shot weighs 16 pounds (7.26 kg).

Heptathlon
The women's version of the decathlon is the heptathlon. Women compete in seven events: 100-meter (110-yd.) hurdles, high jump, shot put, 200 meters (220 yd.), long jump, javelin, and 800 meters (880 yd.).

The Pole Vault
The pole is about 16 feet (5 m) long and is made of fiberglass. Top pole vaulters have managed to clear heights of about 20 feet (6 m).

Once he has pushed off from the ground, the vaulter hangs from the pole to make it bend.

Vaulters often put tape around the pole to help them get a good grip.

The vaulter starts running toward the crossbar with the pole held almost upright. As he runs, he lowers the end of the pole toward the ground.

The crossbar is placed on supports on the uprights. It is winched up to the required height.

As the pole straightens, it powers the vaulter upward. He does a handstand and prepares to throw himself over the crossbar.

The landing mat is filled with foam.

The vaulter plants the pole in the vaulting box – a sloping metal box set into the ground in front of the landing mat.

GYMNASTICS

If you can do a cartwheel or a handstand or play leapfrog, then you are a gymnast! Being a champion gymnast requires complete dedication and a mixture of grace and strength. Competitors have to be able to somersault and spin across the floor exercise mat and leap on and off the apparatus with amazing confidence.

Female gymnasts wear skintight, long-sleeved leotards made of stretchy material. They let them move around easily.

Gymnasts keep their hair tied back so that it does not get in the way.

Competitors put chalk on their hands to help them grip.

Rhythmic All-Around

Rhythmic gymnastics was first included in the Olympics in Los Angeles in 1984. Competitors do jumps, skips, hops, and spirals to music, using ropes, hoops, balls, clubs, and ribbons. The ribbon the gymnasts use is 20 feet (6 m) long and is very hard to control.

The beam is padded and covered in suede. It is 16.5 feet (5 m) long, 4 feet (1.2 m) high and only 4 inches (10 cm) wide.

Women's Floor Exercise

Gymnasts perform the most incredible tumbles, handstands, and cartwheels as they spring across the floor.

*is gymnast
ows remarkable
lance as she
lds her body in a
amatic arched
position.*

Age Advantage
The younger you are, the easier it is to do basic gymnastic positions, like splits. Many top gymnasts are only in their early teens.

Full Flight
Gymnasts swing around and around on the uneven bars, then let go to move from one bar to another.

Hanging Around
Male gymnasts have to do handstands while competing on the rings. Performing a move like this requires great strength.

Swinging, Jumping, and Balancing
As well as performing floor exercises, gymnasts compete on many different pieces of apparatus.

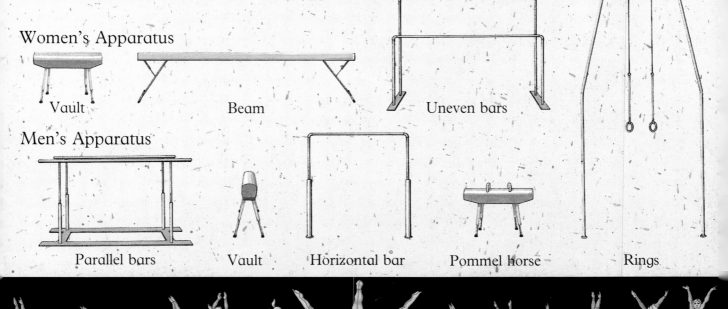

Women's Apparatus

Vault   Beam   Uneven bars

Men's Apparatus

Parallel bars   Vault   Horizontal bar   Pommel horse   Rings

MARTIAL ARTS

All over the world, sports have developed from people fighting each other. Most of these sports are now controlled so that the contestants hurt themselves as little as possible – boxers wear padded gloves, and fencers have protective tips on the ends of their swords. Some martial arts of the East, such as judo and karate, are only meant to be used as a method of self-defense and self-control.

Sumo Wrestling

In Japan, top sumo wrestlers are treated like superstars. In a fight, the wrestlers use their enormous bulk to try to push each other right out of the combat circle. Hawaiian-born wrestler Konishiki, known as "the Dump Truck," weighs about 500 pounds (225 kg). It would take nine small girls to equal his weight. The wrestlers eat huge amounts of a high-protein stew, called *chanko-nabe*.

Each contestant attempts to get the other off balance in order to throw him or her to the floor.

Judo

The aim of judo, which means "the soft way," is not to hurt your opponent but to show skill in carrying out the different judo throws.

A judo mat has to be thick enough to absorb the weight of falling bodies. The first technique beginners are taught is how to fall without injuring themselves.

Belt Up!

The color of the belt worn by judo competitors shows how good they are. The grades range from white to yellow, orange, green, blue, and brown. Then comes the famous black belt. Masters of the sport can progress beyond the black belt to a white-and-red-striped belt, then to a red belt, and finally back to a white belt again!

Fencing

There are three swords used in fencing: the foil, épée, and sabre. All of them have protective tips, but contestants still wear strong clothes and a face mask to keep them from coming to any harm.

Only the tip of the foil can be used to score points.

Kite Fighting

One combat sport that is unlikely to hurt anybody is kite fighting. Flyers use their kites to move the special glass-coated line backward and forward over their opponent's line. This cuts the line and sends the enemy kite spiraling out of control.

The judo costume of jacket, trousers, and belt is called the judogi.

The jacket has to be very tough because of all the tugging that goes on during a bout.

Boxing

Many of the world's top boxers have been Olympic medal winners. The most famous boxer of all time is Muhammad Ali. He won a gold medal at the 1960 Olympics in Rome, Italy.

Competitors go barefoot on the mat, but they have to cover their feet as soon as they leave it.

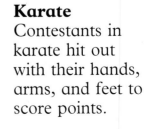

Karate

Contestants in karate hit out with their hands, arms, and feet to score points.

ARCHERY

Hitting a target with an arrow, a dart, or a bullet requires a lot of skill. To fire an arrow from a bow, you also need to be strong enough to pull back the bowstring, which is incredibly tight. Modern target archery bows do not look much like the traditional type of bow used by the legendary archer Robin Hood. They are made of advanced materials such as carbon fiber and have a sight and stabilizers.

Stabilizer

Arrows have a sharp metal tip at the front and a groove at the back that slots over the bowstring.

Stabilizer

Field Archery

In field archery, the archers have to move around a course shooting at different-sized targets from unknown distances. The instinctive bows used in barebow field archery do not have any sights or stabilizers, so they look more like a traditional bow.

Instinctive bow

An archer keeps arrows in a holster-style pouch, or quiver, which hangs from a belt around the waist.

The shorter the bow, the faster the arrow flies, but longer bows are easier to control.

Target Archery

In target archery, competitors shoot at one target from various distances.

The sight is adjusted so that when the archer lines it up with the target, the arrow should hit the place he or she is aiming at.

Shooting

Rifle-shooting competitors fire at unmoving targets. Rapid-fire pistol shooting targets are only turned toward the competitor for a few seconds. Free pistol shooters have two and a half hours to fire 60 shots at unmoving targets. Competitors at a clay pigeon shoot use shotguns to fire at airborne clay targets.

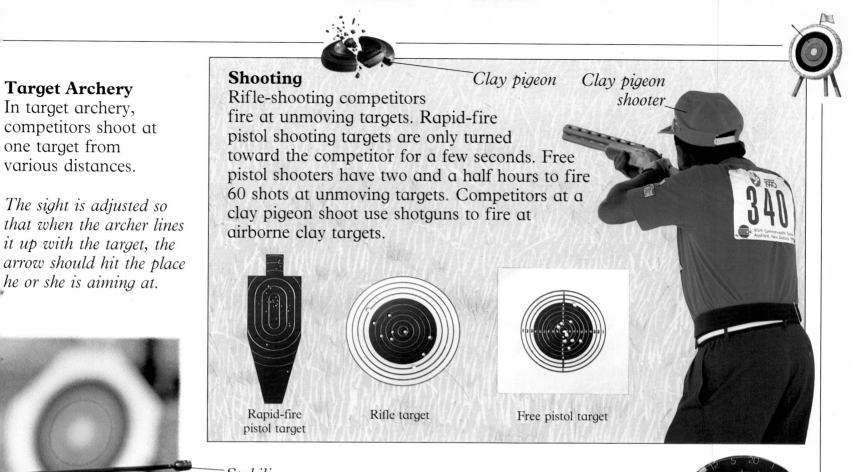

Clay pigeon

Clay pigeon shooter

Rapid-fire pistol target

Rifle target

Free pistol target

Stabilizers are attached to the bow to help keep it steady while shooting.

Darts

Players throw darts at numbered segments on a round board. The aim of the game is to work down from 301, 501, or 1,001 to zero. So your math has to be pretty efficient to figure out the score!

Darts have a sharp tip, so be careful when you take aim.

On Target

Archery targets, known as butts, are made of straw ropes that are stitched together. Colored paper or canvas targets are pinned to the butts. The nearer an arrow lands to the center of the target, the higher the score.

GOLF

There are a number of sports that involve throwing or rolling a ball – bowling, for example, and the French game of boules. There are other sports, such as golf or snooker, in which you use a stick to hit a ball. On a golf course, golfers use as few shots as possible to hit the ball from the tee, down the fairway, onto the green, and into the hole. Golfers have major obstacles to deal with, including trees, rivers, and big ditches, called bunkers, full of sand.

To hit the ball hard, golfers raise the club up behind them. Then they take a big swing at the ball so that the club ends up behind the back.

Clubs with angled metal heads, known as irons, are used to make most of the shots.

Golfers wear shoes with spikes on the soles to help keep them steady when they swing at the ball.

Bowling Sports

In bowling, boules, and bowls, the aim of the game is to hit a target with a ball. In bowls, players roll the ball as near as possible to the target ball, or jack. Boules players throw the ball toward the jack. Bowlers roll the ball down an alley and try to knock over the pins standing at the end.

Jack

Boules is played on a gravel surface.

Bowlers play on a wooden alley.

Bowls is normally played on grass.

Brunswick
GRM2688
Black Beauty

Pin

Jack

Playing a Hole

For his first shot, the player balances the ball on a holder, called a tee peg.

Play starts with a drive, or tee shot, onto the fairway.

The fairway is a long stretch of short grass.

A player needs to have a firm grip on the club. Wearing a glove on one hand helps.

One of the first techniques that golfers learn is how to hold the club correctly.

Golfing Hall of Fame

Here are some great golfing champions and their years at the top.

Bobby Jones
1920s

Ben Hogan
1940s and 1950s

Jack Nicklaus
1960s and 1970s

Seve Ballesteros
1970s and 1980s

Winning Team

Fanny Sunneson is a caddy for champion golfer Nick Faldo. Top caddies do more than carry the clubs – they know the world's major courses well and make suggestions on how to play each hole.

Wood

Irons

Putter

Choosing a Club

There are three types of golf clubs: woods, irons, and putters. Woods are used for hitting the ball a long way. Irons are best for middle-distance shots up the fairway. Putters are designed for hitting the ball across the green and into the hole.

Snooker

Snooker is played on a large cloth-covered table with six pockets. Players use a wooden cue to make a white ball hit the colored balls. The aim is to knock these balls into the pockets.

The golfer hits the ball down the fairway, trying to avoid the long grass, trees, and bunkers. Unfortunately, this ball lands in a bunker!

Finally the ball is pitched onto the green. The green is a smooth, grassy area where the golfer putts the ball into the hole.

TENNIS

Games such as tennis, squash, and table tennis all involve hitting a ball between players. Tennis, in various forms, has been played for centuries, and its popularity continues to grow. It can be played indoors or outdoors by two people (singles), four people (doubles), and by men and women together (mixed doubles).

1930s wooden tennis racket

Tennis Hall of Fame
The championships held at the All England Tennis and Croquet Club, Wimbledon, London, are considered the greatest in the world. In their day, these players made the event their own.

Elizabeth Ryan's record of 19 titles, set between 1914 and 1934, was only beaten by Billie Jean King in 1979.

Fred Perry's record of three wins in a row between 1934 and 1936 was broken by Bjorn Borg in 1979.

Modern rackets are designed by computer and are made of very strong, light materials such as graphite or fiberglass.

Players wear different types of shoes depending on the playing surface. Soles have raised dots for grass play.

Line judge

Wristbands and headbands help soak up sweat during long, energetic games.

Tennis balls are made of hollow rubber covered with a fluffy layer of wool and synthetic fibers.

Pelota
Pelota players use a wicker scoop to throw a ball against the walls of a court. The ball can travel at over 180 miles (290 km) an hour.

Hit Records
Tennis player Steve Denton hit the fastest-ever recorded serve of 138 miles (222 km) an hour.

The fastest speed that a squash ball has traveled is 144 miles (232 km) an hour.

Two table-tennis players rallied for a record-breaking 172 shots in 60 seconds.

Badminton is played with shuttlecocks. They can travel at nearly 125 miles (200 km) an hour.

This player is making a forehand shot. The three basic tennis strokes are serve, forehand, and backhand.

Table Tennis
Table tennis was originally played with simple wooden bats. When the bats were given a rubber covering, the players were able to spin the ball. The game then became more exciting and grew increasingly popular with players and spectators.

The Court
Tennis court surfaces include grass, clay, concrete, and asphalt.

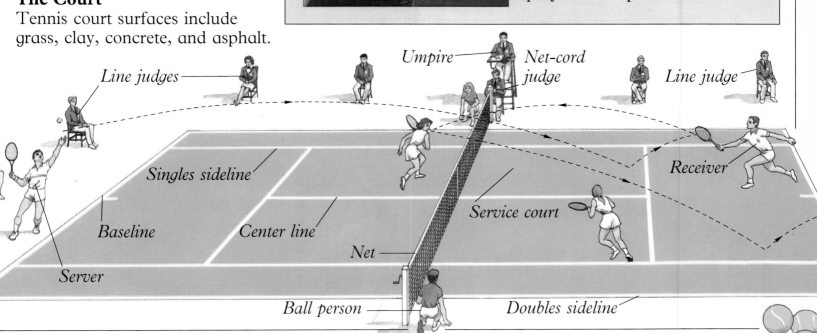

Line judges

Umpire

Net-cord judge

Line judge

Singles sideline

Receiver

Baseline

Center line

Service court

Net

Server

Ball person

Doubles sideline

BASKETBALL

The team games of handball, volleyball, and basketball are all action packed and high scoring, and the players have to move incredibly quickly around the court. In basketball, two teams of five players try to throw the ball through the other team's basket. Players cannot run with the ball or kick it, but they are allowed to dribble, pass, throw, or roll it, so they have to be extremely agile and very accurate – and it helps to be tall, too!

Players wear sleeveless shirts so that they can move their arms easily as they reach up above their heads to catch the ball.

Court Magicians
The Magicians of Basketball, as the world-famous Harlem Globetrotters are called, have been entertaining fans with their amazing trick shots for over 70 years.

Fashionable Feet
Famous players like Michael Jordan help to design their own basketball shoes, which are then produced for sale to the public.

Ankle support

Foot support

Air-filled sole

Michael Jordan

Players often throw the ball at the backboard to try to get it to rebound into the basket.

A basketball has a rough surface so that players can get a good grip on it no matter how sweaty their hands are!

The top of the basket is over 10 feet (3 m) off the ground, but some players can jump high enough to drop, or dunk, the ball straight into the net.

Basketball has to be played on a hard surface so that the ball bounces well. A polished wooden surface is ideal.

Team Handball

Team handball is a fast and furious game that is a mix of basketball and soccer. The ball moves down the court in the same way as it does in basketball, but points are scored by throwing the ball into a goal.

Volleyball

Volleyball is played by two teams of six players on a hard court. Players use their hands to hit the ball over a high net. They try to keep the ball off the ground for as long as possible. Beach volleyball is played on sand on beaches everywhere in the United States, where it is a popular summer pastime.

Dribble and Shoot

The player gets the ball, but he cannot move unless he bounces it. This is known as dribbling.

He dribbles around an opponent.

He picks up the ball and jumps for the basket.

SOCCER

Soccer is the most popular team game in the world. Eleven players on each side attempt to kick the ball into the other team's goal. The only member of the team who is allowed to touch the ball with his hands is the goalkeeper. Teams play for 45 minutes and have a 15-minute rest at halftime. Then they swap ends and play for another, exhausting half lasting 45 minutes.

Sporting Supporters
You can buy child-sized versions of your national soccer team's "strip," or outfit. But these strips change every few years, so keeping up to date with the latest style can be expensive.

The captain of a soccer team wears a colored armband.

Players can be identified by the large number on the back of their shirt.

Massive Crowd
The world's largest soccer stadium is the Estadio Maracana, in Rio de Janeiro, Brazil. The stadium can hold up to 165,000 spectators.

Balls used in top matches are made of leather panels, stitched together over an inflatable rubber inner ball.

Action from Goal to Goal
A soccer field is usually between 100 and 130 yards (90 and 120 m) from end to end.

The goalkeeper kicks the ball to a teammate.

This player runs with the ball before passing.

Goal line

The World Cup

Every four years, the world's greatest soccer-playing countries compete for the World Cup. In 1970, the Brazilian team was allowed to keep the original cup after winning the competition for the third time. Teams now play for a new World Cup.

Soccer Hall of Fame

Here are 11 of the game's greatest players and the countries they played for.

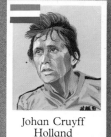

Gordon Banks England	Franco Baresi Italy	Franz Beckenbauer Germany
George Best Northern Ireland	Bobby Charlton England	Johan Cruyff Holland
Eusebio Spain	Diego Maradona Argentina	Bobby Moore England
Pelé Brazil	Frank Rijkaard Holland	

A soccer player's "strip" – shorts and shirt – has changed a lot over the years. Shorts have gone from baggy to tight and back to baggy again.

Players often wear shin guards underneath their socks to protect their legs during heavy tackles.

Soccer shoes are very light to allow the player to run fast and to give him or her a good feel for the ball.

Corner flag

Attacker beats defender . . . then goalkeeper . . . and it's a goal!

Linesman

The referee makes sure the teams play by the rules.

The attacking players outwit the defense and move the ball up the field.

Goalkeeper

RUGBY AND AMERICAN FOOTBALL

The games of rugby and American football involve lots of physical contact. The players run with an oval ball and have to touch down over a line to score. They can also kick the ball between the tall goal posts to score points. The big difference is that rugby players are not allowed to pass the ball forward, while football players can pass in any direction.

Football players wear a plastic helmet and face mask. Inside the helmet, lots of small cushions fit snugly around the head.

American footballs have pointed ends to make them easier to throw.

Under his lightweight shirt, this player has a plastic rib protector and huge shoulder and chest pads.

This player has a towel attached to his belt. He uses it to wipe his hands before each play.

Players wear tight, knee-length pants that lace up the front.

Hip, groin, and thigh pads are worn underneath the pants.

Dressing for Action
American football players have to be well protected because they are allowed to make physical contact away from the ball.

American Football Field
Football players play mainly on artificial turf, which is laid on top of a solid concrete base.

American football shoes are lightweight to help the players run and turn quickly.

Starting lineup

All sorts of pulling and tugging goes on in the rugby scrum, so players often wrap tape around their head to protect their ears.

Rugby players protect their teeth with a special plastic gum shield.

Players wear a basic outfit of cotton shirt and shorts.

Rugby balls have rounded ends.

Australian Rules
Australia-rules football is played by two teams of 18 on an oval field with four upright posts at each end. Players can kick, punch, and run with the ball, but it has to touch the ground, usually by bouncing, every 11 yards (10 m).

Rugby Field
Rugby players usually play on grass field. They often come off the field looking as though they have just taken a mud bath.

Starting lineup

Rugby boots are made of tough leather and have studs on the soles to cope with slippery mud.

The quarterback waits to receive the ball.

The American Snap
In the snap, players line up opposite each other. The team with the ball passes it to their quarterback, who determines the next play.

The Rugby Scrum
During a scrum, the ball is put into a huddle of players from both teams. The teams push each other backward. The players in the scrum use their feet to push the ball out to their scrum half.

The scrum half waits for a chance to grab the ball.

BASEBALL

Baseball, softball, rounders, and cricket have all developed from a basic bat-and-ball game that has been played since ancient times. All of these games involve hitting a ball with a bat and running between or around bases. The fielders have to return the ball in order to stop the runner's progress.

Batter's helmet   *Fielder's cap*

The umpire-in-chief kneels right behind the catcher and decides if the balls have been pitched correctly.

Because the umpire is so close to the play, he has to wear a protective mask.

The catcher wears a face guard, a chest protector, and knee and shin guards.

The catcher's padded mitt helps him catch the speeding ball if the batter misses it.

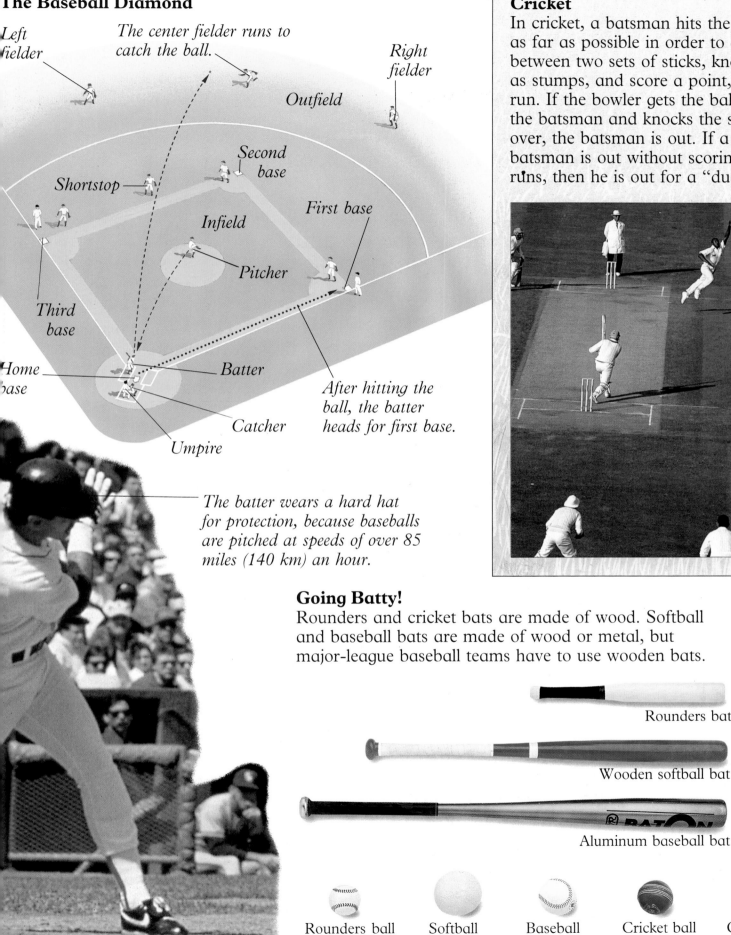

The Baseball Diamond

Left fielder

The center fielder runs to catch the ball.

Right fielder

Outfield

Second base

Shortstop

First base

Infield

Third base

Pitcher

Home base

Batter

After hitting the ball, the batter heads for first base.

Catcher

Umpire

The batter wears a hard hat for protection, because baseballs are pitched at speeds of over 85 miles (140 km) an hour.

Cricket

In cricket, a batsman hits the ball as far as possible in order to dash between two sets of sticks, known as stumps, and score a point, or run. If the bowler gets the ball past the batsman and knocks the stumps over, the batsman is out. If a batsman is out without scoring any runs, then he is out for a "duck."

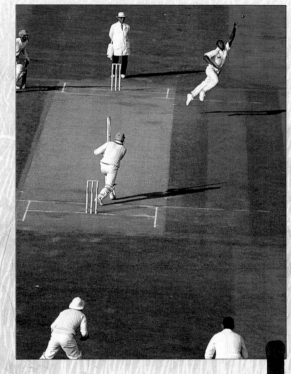

Going Batty!

Rounders and cricket bats are made of wood. Softball and baseball bats are made of wood or metal, but major-league baseball teams have to use wooden bats.

Rounders bat

Wooden softball bat

Aluminum baseball bat

Cricket bat

Rounders ball   Softball   Baseball   Cricket ball   Cricket bat

ICE HOCKEY

Ice hockey, like soccer, involves scoring goals by shooting an object into an opponent's net. But ice hockey players don't play with a ball – they use a rubber disk, called a puck, and they hit it with a stick. The game is fast and furious and very physical. The players speed across the ice and crash against each other. Roller hockey and field hockey are exciting, too, and players show great skill as they control the ball while moving at high speed.

Dangerous Position
The goalkeeper needs all the protection he can get when faced with a dangerous flying puck. He wears a chest protector under his shirt, a face mask, and leg guards.

Crushed Ice
An ice hockey game is split into three periods of 20 minutes. The ice takes a real bashing during a game. To make the surface smooth again, a resurfacing machine trundles around the rink between periods.

Crashing Around
The rink is surrounded by boards over a yard high. Spectators sitting just behind the boards are only inches from the action as the players crash into each other and the sideboards.

There are six members on each team.

The goal is not very big – just 4 feet (1.2 m) high and 6 feet (1.8 m) wide.

Field Hockey

There are 11 players on a field hockey team. The game is usually played on grass. The head of a field hockey stick is tiny compared to that of an ice hockey stick.

Roller Hockey

Roller hockey is played by teams of five. The players wear in-line skates or roller skates with a wheel on each corner.

In-line skates have four wheels in a row and, as with ice hockey skates, you need a good sense of balance to use them.

Players wear all sorts of protective gear under their clothing, as well as padded gloves and helmets.

Sinful Behavior

When players disobey the rules, the referee sends them off the ice and into the penalty box for up to ten minutes.

KOSKINEN

The blades on ice hockey skates are shorter than those on figure skates. This makes them safer and more maneuverable.

Ice hockey sticks are 53 inches (135 cm) long. Players are not supposed to swing their sticks above shoulder height – if they do, they get sent to the penalty box.

FIGURE SKATING

World-class figure skaters have to carry out extremely complicated, and dangerous, moves as part of their routines. Perhaps their greatest skill is that they make it look so easy. These skaters need a good sense of balance and plenty of confidence. They add speed, grace, strength, and dancing ability to these qualities in order to create the most breathtaking routines. Speed skaters also show amazing control on the ice as they power around frozen tracks at up to 30 miles (50 km) an hour.

Figure skaters perform all sorts of twisting moves on the ice, often while skating very fast.

Skaters have to train constantly to achieve the level of fitness needed to make such physically demanding moves look effortless.

Speed Skating
Speed skaters race around the track in pairs, but they are actually racing against the clock rather than each other. They take swinging steps, throwing their arms from side to side to increase their speed. Their skintight suits and hats help them slice through the air.

Boots give plenty of ankle support.

The skates lace up from toe to ankle for a perfect fit.

Cutting Edge
The blades on figure skates are grooved in the middle. This means that whichever way the skater is leaning, he or she is still balanced on a sharp cutting edge.

Making Moves

There are three different types of figure skating competitions – single skating, pair skating, and ice dancing. In all three, skaters perform routines containing certain set moves as well as routines containing steps they have chosen themselves.

Single skating

Pair skating

Ice dancing

Some ice dance costumes are striking – they are designed to complement the music to which the dancers skate.

Up in the Air

This skater is doing a double Salchow jump. The skater jumps off the ice and does a double twist in the air before landing. This jump is named after Ulrich Salchow, who won the first men's Olympic figure skating gold medal in 1908.

You can see how complicated these twists and turns are by looking at the marks the blades cut into the surface of the ice.

Perfect Partnership

In figure skating, the judges award marks out of six, depending on how good they think a performance is. In 1984, ice dancers Jayne Torvill and Christopher Dean made skating history when they became the first skaters ever to be awarded a row of nine perfect sixes at the Olympic Games.

6.0 6.0 6.0 6.0 6.0 6.0 6.0 6.0 6.0

SKIING

The main things that skiing, ski jumping, and bobsledding have in common are snow, ice, speed, and danger. Downhill skiers reach speeds of over 60 miles (100 km) an hour as they fly down a mountain. Slalom skiers do not travel quite so fast, but they have to twist and turn around marker poles with incredible agility.

Downhill racers wear protective helmets because skiing is extremely dangerous at high speeds.

Ski poles help skiers turn and keep their balance. Downhill skiers use poles that curve around the body.

Ski boots are made of strong plastic and give the foot and ankle plenty of support.

Skiing Events
In skiing there are seven different types of competitive events.

Snowboarding
A snowboard is a lot wider than a ski. Boarders do not use ski poles. Straps on the board fasten over the tops of their boots, and they stand sideways, like a surfer. They wear wild clothes and perform amazing jumps.

Skiers weave through a series of poles.

A combination of downhill and slalom skiing

Downhill   Slalom   Giant slalom   Ski jumping

Ski Jumping

A ski jump can be a terrifying 200 feet (60 m) high. Judges in a tower give points for each skier's performance, taking into account the style and length of the jump.

Racers wear skintight suits that do not catch the wind as they rush down the mountain.

The undersides of the skis are coated in wax to help them slide over the snow.

Bobsled and Luge

A luge has no steering or brakes. A bobsled has a fiberglass shell, a steerable front runner, and a brake that digs into the ice. Both speed down a treacherous icy track with high, curved sides.

Luge

Two-man bobsled

Skis and Boots

Cross-country equipment is much lighter than that used for downhill skiing.

Downhill skis

Cross-country skis

The toe of a cross-country shoe is attached to a single binding on the ski.

Cross-country is done across uneven, snow-covered countryside.

Freestylers specialize in either ballet, jumping, or racing down bumpy slopes, called mogul fields.

Competitors ski cross-country and fire at targets along the way.

Clamps, called bindings, hold the boot onto the ski. The bindings release the ski during a fall.

Cross-country shoes

Downhill boots

Cross-country   Freestyle   Biathlon

THREE-DAY EVENT

Dressage hat

Endurance hat

Show-jumping hat

Competing in the three-day event is the ultimate test of a person's horsemanship. The first day's riding takes place in the hushed dressage arena. The second day's challenge is carried out on the long and tiring endurance course. Then, on the third day, horse and rider have to show themselves to be strong enough to clear the jumps on the tricky, winding show-jumping course.

Jumps can be up to 4 feet (1.2 m) tall, which is probably as tall as you!

Riders get penalty points if their horse knocks down part of an obstacle or refuses to jump.

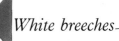

White breeches

Polo
Polo is known as hockey on horseback. Two teams of four players thunder up and down the polo field. They attempt to use their long-handled mallets to hit the small polo ball between the goal posts. The owner of a polo team has to be rich, because polo ponies are very expensive.

Fancy gate   Hog's back

Water jump

Stone wall

Clearing the Jumps

The show-jumping course is made up of between 10 and 12 different jumps.

The rider leans forward in the saddle to help the horse balance as it powers its way over the jump.

The reins are attached to the bit. When the rider pulls on the left or right rein, the horse turns in that direction.

Red hunting jacket

The leather bridle holds a metal bit in the horse's mouth.

The same horse takes part in each stage of the three-day event.

131

Dressage

In the dressage competition, riders aim to show that their horses follow their commands absolutely. At first it may look boring, but if you look closely, you can see how accurately the horse stops, starts, and changes speed and direction.

Endurance

The speed and endurance course involves riding across roads, paths, and fields. Competitors ride over jumps, up and down steep slopes, and over, or sometimes through, water. The course is 15 miles (25 km) long and is muddy and dangerous.

CYCLING

There is more to riding a bike than going from place to place. Mountain-bike racers tackle impossibly steep hills and ride through mud and water. Road racers cover enormous distances and ride for days on end. Track racers hurtle around an arena at speeds of up to 50 miles (80 km) an hour, without any brakes or gears.

Track Racing
Track racers compete on an oval track with banked sides, called a velodrome. The arrival of the futuristic Lotus Superbike in Barcelona, Spain, for the 1992 Olympics put the sport in headlines all over the world.

Triathlon
Triathletes swim, cycle, and run, all in one event. In the Iron Man, the longest of the triathlon events, competitors have to cycle 112 miles (180 km). Triathlon bikes have handlebars with elbow pads to support the rider.

Road racers should wear helmets, but some riders complain that they make them too hot.

Mountain-bike Racing
Mountain bikes are very sturdy machines with rugged, knobbly tires, strong brakes, and lots of gears. These bikes are built to be ridden off the road, up steep slopes, and through extremely rough terrain. An off-road race can get pretty tough, so bike and rider have to be in peak condition if they are going to finish.

Cyclists wear skintight shorts and shirts. These keep the rider warm and streamlined.

The Great Race

The Tour de France is the greatest road race of all. Every year, hundreds of riders cover over 2,000 miles (3,220 km) as they snake their way across France. The top three riders are awarded a colored jersey at the end of each day to show what part of the race they have done well in.

Yellow jersey (leading rider)   *Polka-dot jersey (most climbing points)*   *Green jersey (most sprint points)*

Changing Gear

All bikes have the same basic shape, but wheel, frame, saddle, and handlebar styles vary.

Mountain bike

Life on the Road

Road-race riders avoid stopping at all costs. They eat and drink on the move, and simple repairs are carried out by mechanics hanging out of cars that speed alongside the bikes.

Road-racing bike

Riders apply special oils to their legs to keep the muscles and knee joints warm.

The riders shave their legs to make it easier to apply protective oils to their skin.

Time-trial bike

Racers wear special shoes that clip onto the bike's pedals. This helps the rider pull the pedals up as well as push them down.

Track-racing bike

MOTOR SPORTS

When you watch a motor race, your senses are bombarded by the event. The engines roar so loudly that you feel the ground shake. You smell burning rubber as tires spin on tarmac. You watch mechanics desperately trying to keep their machines working. For both the drivers and the spectators, there is no doubt that motor sports are among the most exciting sporting experiences in the world.

Rallying
Rally cars are based on road cars. Each car has a navigator and a driver. The navigator reads a map and, because the cars are so noisy, uses a microphone to tell the driver which way to go.

During a race, repairs are done in the pits. Mechanics work as fast as they can to get the car back into the race.

A driver wears a helmet fitted with a microphone so that it is possible to speak to the pit crew at all times.

A tire change takes under eight seconds. The tires are held on by special nuts that can be undone easily.

This car has wings at the front and back. At high speed, air rushes over the wings. The pressure of this air keeps the car on the ground.

Drag Racing
Drag-racing cars are designed to go as fast as possible in a straight line. They reach speeds of 290 miles (470 km) an hour.

The car speeds down a track 440 yards (400 m) long.

Motorcycling

Racing motorcycles are extremely fast and have wide tires and curved windshields. The sport looks very dramatic because the bikes corner at such an amazing angle to the track that the rider's knees almost scrape the ground!

Speedway

Speedway bikes race anticlockwise around an oval track with a loose, dry surface. The bikes corner at speeds of up to 70 miles (110 km) an hour. But because they do not have brakes, the riders slide the bikes around the corners to slow down.

These mechanics are wearing flameproof headgear because they are refueling the car.

During a race, the tires get very hot. This makes them sticky and helps the car grip the track.

Double Record

British driver Nigel Mansell is one of the greatest racing drivers of the 1980s and 1990s. In 1993 he became the only driver in history to be both Formula One and American IndyCar champion at the same time.

The only way of slowing the car down quickly once it crosses the finishing line . . .

. . . is by releasing a parachute!

Finishing flag

SWIMMING

An Olympic-size swimming pool is 55 yards (50 m) long, with eight lanes for the competitors to swim up and down in. Depending on whether they do the front crawl, backstroke, breaststroke, or butterfly, Olympic swimmers can compete over distances ranging from 55 to 1,650 yards (50 to 1,500 m). These swimmers train so hard that they spend most of their waking hours in a pool.

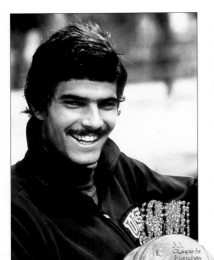

Super Swimmer
In 1972, Mark Spitz made sporting history when he became the first competitor ever to win seven gold medals at one Olympics.

A swimming cap keeps hair out of this swimmer's face. Loose, long hair could even slow a swimmer down.

The butterfly is the second-fastest swimming stroke after the front crawl. Top butterfly swimmers cover 110 yards (100 m) in under 60 seconds.

Water Polo
Water polo is an exhausting game. Players need to be very confident swimmers because they have to control the ball with one hand. They are not allowed to punch the ball or to touch the bottom of the pool. Teams are identified by their white or blue caps. Goalkeepers wear red caps.

Front crawl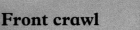

Backstroke

Breaststroke

Butterfly

Tumble Turns

To save time, swimmers turn underwater at the end of a length. When you roll over, water goes up your nose, so swimmers breathe out through their noses as they turn.

Diving

Competition diving is done from springboards or high, rigid platforms. Divers leave the board forward, backward, or sometimes from a handstand. Then they bend double, go into a tuck, or even do twists and somersaults before entering the water.

10-m (30-ft.) platform

7.5-m (25-ft.) platform

This swimmer is doing the butterfly. The butterfly stroke developed about 60 years ago when swimmers doing the breaststroke started to lift their arms out of the water.

5-m (16.5-ft.) platform

3-m (10-ft.) springboard

Most racers wear goggles so that they can see where they are the minute they enter the water.

1-m (3.3-ft.) springboard

Special ropes separate the lanes and stop the splashing and waves made by each swimmer from reaching the competitors on either side.

The front crawl is the fastest stroke.

The breaststroke is the oldest and slowest stroke.

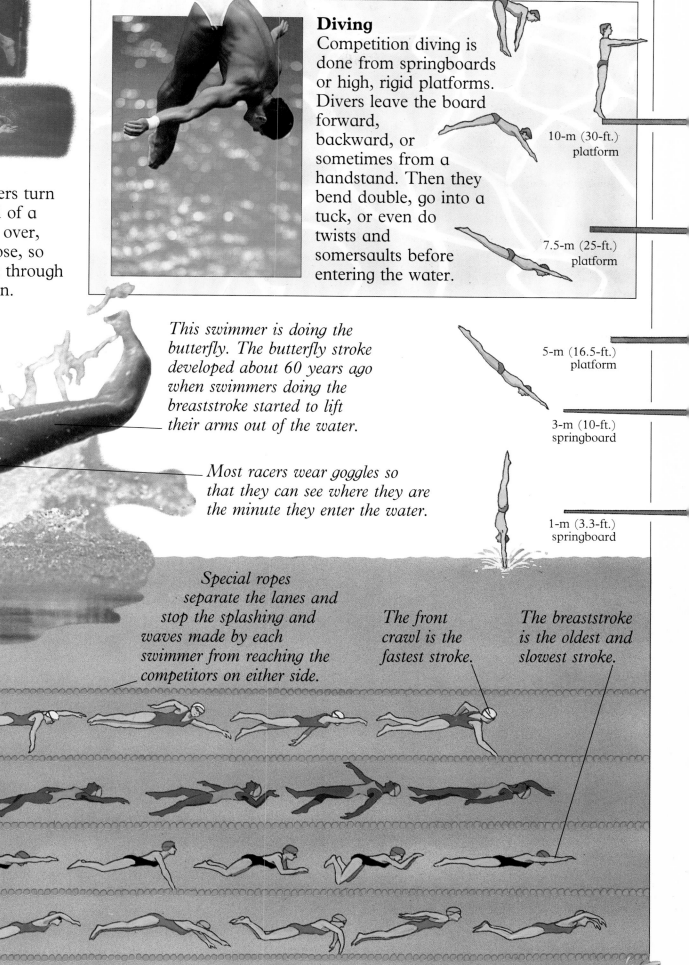

ROWING

On rivers, lakes, and the sea, you can employ one of the world's most incredible engines to power a craft across the water. That engine is – you! Using either paddles or oars, you can get enormous satisfaction as your boat or canoe cuts through the water. You can also hoist sails to use the natural force of the wind to get a boat on the move.

Sculling

Sculling is different from rowing because the competitors use two short oars (sculls) each rather than one long oar.

The blade is the part of the oar that pushes the water and moves the boat.

The oars are nearly 13 feet (4 m) long. Long oars give greater pulling power and help the boat go faster.

The rower at the front moves the rudder at the other end of the boat by pulling wires with his or her feet.

Competition boats like this one are narrow and light so that they speed through the water.

Metal holders, called oarlocks, hold the oars out over the water.

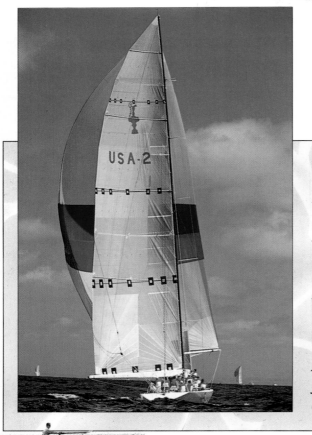

Sailing

Sailing boats of many different sizes take part in competitions. They can sail across oceans or along inland waterways. But they all follow the same basic principle – positioning the sails so that they are filled by the wind. This moves the boat along.

This gigantic America's Cup yacht needs a crew of over ten people.

This Laser 2 sailing dinghy can be sailed by one person. It is small enough to be transported on top of a car.

Canoeing

There are two different types of canoe – a Canadian canoe and a kayak. In a Canadian canoe, you half-kneel and use a single-bladed paddle. You sit in a kayak and use a paddle with a blade on each end.

Canadian canoe

Kayak

Slalom canoeists have to steer their way through a series of green gates. But if the gate is red, the canoeist has to go past it and paddle back up through it.

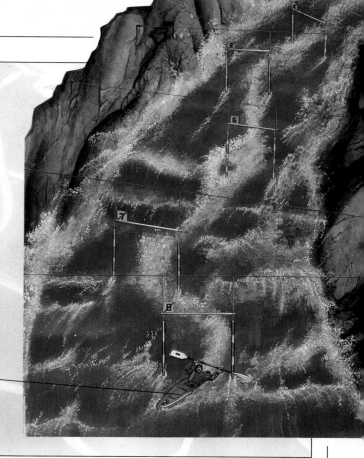

The oarsman at the back, called the stroke, sets the rhythm for the whole boat.

This indicator shows the direction of the rudder below. When the rudder is moved to the left or right, the boat turns in the same direction.

The Boat Race

The rowing race between the English universities of Oxford and Cambridge first took place in 1829. The teams of eight rowers and a cox do battle every year over a 4.2-mile (6.78-km) stretch of the river Thames.

The cox steers the boat and helps the team row together.

WINDSURFING

The sea is one of the world's greatest natural sporting facilities. You can ride the waves on a board, with a sail, or while being towed behind a boat. Windsurfing and surfing can be enjoyed during a vacation at the beach, but for some people these sports become a way of life as they search for ideal conditions or perfect waves.

One-design Racing
Competitors in the Olympic windsurfing course-racing event all have to use the same type of sail and board.

Plastic battens slide into pockets in the sail to help it keep its shape.

The boom goes around the mast and the sail. The windsurfer pulls on the boom to move the sail around and change direction.

Mast

Board Lengths
Beginners can use a funboard or a mid-length board. Slalom racers use a shorter board. Top slalom, wave, and speed windsurfers often have a board specially made for them.

Windsurfers often sail in cold weather, so they have to wear wetsuits to keep warm.

Funboard

Mid-length board

Slalom board

Custom-made board

Surfing

Surfers use a board to ride enormous waves as they roll toward the shoreline. An ultimate surfing move is to ride along the inside of the wave as the top curls right over you. This is known as riding the tube.

Beginners can ride the waves lying on a body board.

This board is made to jump waves, so it is particularly short and light.

Riding the Wind

Windsurfers can take part in different competitions. They can race around a slalom course, do spectacular wave jumps, or attempt speed records on very narrow boards, called speed needles.

The fin, or skeg, helps to keep the board stable in the water.

Slalom

Wave performance

Speed

Water Skiing

Water skiers are towed behind a boat and use one or two skis. Slalom skiers use one ski and have to swing out behind the towing boat in order to ski around six marker buoys.

WHO'S WHO?

Find out more about the athletes, players and teams featured in Picturepedia Sport.

World of Sport

Cricket: *Salim Malik (Pakistan), Duchess of Norfolk XI vs. Pakistan, Arundel, 1992;* Special Olympics: *Tanni Grey (GB), Barcelona 1992;* Winter Olympics: *Stephane Exartier (France), Albertville 1992;* Runner: *William Tanui (Kenya), IAAF/Mobil Grand Prix, Lausanne, 1992;* Show-jumper: *Mark Todd (NZ) on Kleenex Face the Music, The Dubai Eventers Special 1991;* Diver: *Mingxia Fu (China), Barcelona 1992;* Tennis Player: *Steffi Graf (Germany), Wimbledon 1993;* Athlete: *Carl Lewis (USA), Barcelona 1992.*

Running

Relay: *Dennis Mitchell and Carl Lewis (USA), Barcelona 1.992;* Steeplechase: *Kenyans Matthew Birir (1107), Patrick Sang (1138), William Mutwol (1133), Barcelona 1992;* 100 Meters: *Merlene Ottey (Jamaica), World Championships, Tokyo, 1991;* Hurdles: *Colin Jackson (GB), European Championships, Split, 1990;* Start: *Giuseppina Cirulli (Italy), Los Angeles 1984;* Long Distance: *Doina Melinte (Romania), IAAF/Mobil Grand Prix, Stockholm, 1992.*

Decathlon

Pole Vaulter: *Ian Tullett (GB) 1993;* Heptathlon: *Jackie Joyner-Kersee (USA), Seoul 1988.*

Gymnastics

Rhythmic All-Around: *Alexandra Timochenko (EUN), Barcelona 1992;* Beam: *Zsuzsanna Csisztu (Hungary), Seoul 1988;* Uneven Bars: *Li Lu (China), World Champ-ionships, Paris, 1992;* Rings: *Vitaliy Scherbo (EUN), World Championships, Birmingham, 1993.*

Martial Arts

Judo: *Cecile Nowak (France) vs. Ryoko Tamura (Japan), Barcelona 1992.*

Archery

Archery: *Seoul 1988;* Shooting: *The Sultan of Brunei, Commonwealth Games, Auckland, 1990.*

Golf

Golf: *Florence Descampe (Belgium), Dinah Shore Open, Mission Hills, 1993;* Snooker: *Stephen Hendry (GB), World Championships, Sheffield, 1992.*

Tennis

Tennis: *Gretchen Magers (USA), Wimbledon 1989;* Pelota: *Biarritz (France) 1991;* Table Tennis: *Li Huifen (China), English Open Championships, Brighton, 1988.*

Basketball

Basketball: *Golden State Warriors vs. Portland Trailblazers 1991;* Harlem Globetrotters: *Curly Johnson (USA) and fan;* Fashionable Feet: *Michael Jordan (USA) playing for the Chicago Bulls;* Team Handball: *Korea vs. Norway, Barcelona 1992;* Volleyball: *Kent Steffes (USA) playing Pro Beach Volleyball.*

Soccer

Soccer: *British players Gary McAllister in white (Leeds United) and Mark Hughes in red (Manchester United).*

Rugby and American Football

American Football: *Jim Everett (USA), quarterback for the LA Rams;* Rugby: *Christian Strauss (South Africa), European Tour 1992;* The Snap: *Mark Malone (USA), quarterback for the San Diego Chargers;* The Scrum: *England vs. Ireland;* Australian-Rules Football: *Carlton vs. North Melbourne.*

Baseball

Baseball: *Boston Red Sox vs. Milwaukee Brewers 1990;* Cricket: *England vs. Pakistan, Lords 1992.*

Ice Hockey

Ice Hockey: *USA vs. URS, Calgary 1988;* Goalkeeper: *France vs. USA, Albertville 1992;* Roller Hockey: *Holland vs. Portugal, Barcelona 1992.*

Figure Skating

Figure Skating: *Sophie Moniotte and Pascal Lavanchy (France), European Championships, Lausanne, 1992;* Singles: *Chen Lu (China), Albertville 1992;* Pairs: *Cheryl Peake and Andrew Naylor (GB), Skate Electric International, Richmond, 1990;* Ice Dance: *Stefania Calegari and Pasquale Camerlengo (Italy), World Championships, Prague, 1993;* Record Breakers: *Jayne Torvill and Christopher Dean (GB);* Speed Skating: *Emese Hunyady (Austria), Albertville 1992.*

Skiing

Skiing: *Petra Kronberger (Austria), Lake Louise 1992;* Snowboard: *Avoriaz 1991;* Ski Jump: *Calgary 1988;* Luge: *Susi Erdmann (Germany), World Championships 1993;* Bobsled: *Gustav Weder and Donat Acklin (Switzerland), Albertville 1992.*

Three-Day Event

Three-Day Event: *Nicholas Holmes-Smith (Canada) on Espionage, Seoul 1988;* Dressage: *Mary Thomson (GB) on King William, Barcelona 1992;* Endurance: *Vicki Latta (NZ) on Chief, Barcelona 1992;* Polo: *West Palm Beach 1993.*

Cycling

Tour de France: *Riding through Paris;* Life on the Road: *Laudelino Cubino (Spain), Tour de France;* Mountain-bike Racing: *Barrie Clarke (GB), Grundig MTB Championships, Belgium, 1992;* Track Racing: *Chris Boardman (GB), Barcelona 1992.*

Motor Sports

Racing Car: *Danny Sullivan (USA), Indianapolis 500 1986;* Rallying: *Carlos Sainz (Spain) drives a Toyota, RAC Rally, GB, 1991;* Motorcycling: *Wayne Rainey (USA) on the Roberts Yamaha, British Grand Prix, Donington Park, 1992;* Speedway: *Erik Gundersen (Denmark) leads Jimmy Nilsen (Sweden).*

Swimming

Swimming: *Franziska Van Almsick (Germany), European Championships, Sheffield, 1993;* Tumble Turns: *Sharron Davies (GB);* Diver: *Greg Louganis (USA);* Water Polo: *France vs. Greece, Rome 1990.*

Rowing

Rowing: *Coxless four, Salih Hassan, John Garrett, Gavin Stewart and Richard Stanhope (GB), Barcelona 1992.* Sculling: *Single sculls, Juri Jaanson (Estonia), Barcelona 1992;* Sailing: *Americas Cup 1991;* The Boat Race: *Hammersmith 1991.*

Windsurfing

Windsurfing: *Hawaii;* One-design Racing: *Barcelona 1992;* Slalom: *Slalom race, Hawaii 1990;* Wave Performance: *Bjorn Dunkerbeck (Spain), World Championships, Fuerteventura, 1989;* Speed: *Eric Beale (GB), Les Saintes Maries de la Mer 1988;* Surfing: *Justin Strong (South Africa), Jeffrey Bay 1992.*

INDEX

Acknowledgments

Photography: Andy Crawford, The Colour Company, Kevin Mallet, Dave Rudkin.

Additional photography: Philip Gatward, Dave King, Tim Ridley, Chris Stevens.

Illustrations: Roy Flooks, Garden Studios, Linden Artists, Alex Pang.

Thanks to: John Jaques & Son Limited, Lillywhites, Norrie Carr Model Agency, Ocean Leisure, Olympus Sport, Leon Paul, Queens Ice Rink, Scallywags Model Agency, Jeremy Scoones, Tideway Scullers, Slick Willies, Soccer Scene.

Picture credits

Action Plus: 16r, 21c, Chris Barry 33tr, Barrie Clarke 38bl, Mike Hewitt 30c, 42bl, Glyn Kirk 7c, 7bl, 19cr, 38tr, Eileen Langsley 12c, Peter Spurrier 44tl, P. Tarry 6bc, 6cr, George Tiederman 40/1c, Chris Van Lennep 47tc; **Allsport:** 21tc, 22br, 43tc, Bernard Asset 31tc, Chris Barry 33tc, C. Bernhardt 26c, Shaun Botteril 25tc & back jacket, Howard Boylan 8tl, 27c, 41tl, 41tr, 45br, Simon Bruty 6clb, 13cl, 42/3c & back jacket, David Cannon 19cl, Tony Duffy 9tl, 20bc, Stephen Dunn 18cr, Yann Guichaova 9tr, 12cl, 30tr, Mike Hewitt 23tr, Christian Le Bozec 46tr, Ken Levine 22cl, 23c, Caryn Levy 3c & 20/1c, Bob Martin 1c & 37br, 33br, Richard Martin 14/5c, 32/3c, 33tl, Gary Mortimore 7tr, 17tr, Stephen Munday 19tcr, Adrian Murrell 29cr, Jon Nicholson 47c, Mike Powell 6c, 8cr, 30/1bc, 44bl, Ben Radford 24/5c, Pascal Rondeau 32cr & jacket, 35cr, Richard Saker 13tr, Ian Tomlinson 35c, 35tr; Anton Want 33tr; **Colorsport:** 6/7c, Biancotto 47cl, Valerie Desheulles 46/7c, Desheulles/Montiel 47cr, Bryan Yablonsky 28/9c; **Mary Evans:** 4cl & 10tl; **Guildford Spectrum:** 32tr; **Hulton:** 8cl, 8bl, 15crb, 16tl, 19tl, 19tcl, 20cla, 20c; **Image Bank:** Giuliano Colliva 24cl, Paolo Curto 42tr, Tom King 7tc; **Grafton M. Smith** endpapers; **Bob Langrish:** 36cr, 36/7c & jacket, 37tr; **Popperfoto:** 42tl; **Mark Shearman:** 10/11c; **Sporting Pictures:** Giuseppina Cirulli 4cla, 8br, 6tl, 7br, 9cl & jacket, 9cr, 11tl, 14cl, 20clb, 22/3tc, 27tr, 27bl, 27br, 31c, 34cl & jacket, 35tl, 38/9c, 39cl, 41c, 41br.

Every effort has been made to trace the copyright holders, and we apologize in advance for any unintentional omissions. We would be pleased to insert the appropriate acknowledgments in any subsequent edition of this publication.

| t – top | l – left | a – above |
| b – below | r – right | c – center |